# HOW TO OVERCOME FEAR

*(Tips for Removing Fears, Anxieties, Worries, Nervousness and Phobias)*

**Er. M.K. Gupta**

**PUSTAK MAHAL®**

*Publishers*
**PUSTAK MAHAL®**

***Administrative office and sale centre***
J-3/16, Daryaganj, New Delhi-110002
☎ 011-23276539, 23272783, 23272784, 23260518
*E-mail:* info@pustakmahal.com • *Website:* www.pustakmahal.com

***Branches***
**Bengaluru:** ☎ 080-22234025, 40912845
*E-mail:* pustakmahalblr@gmail.com

**Mumbai:** ☎ 022-22010941, 22053387
*E-mail:* unicornbooksmumbai@gmail.com



ISBN 978-81-223-0050-5

**Edition: 2021**



***Printed at:*** Radha Offset, Delhi

# *Preface*

Fear is said to be one of the deadliest enemies of mankind. But the most surprising thing is that this enemy is created by man himself out of his own mind. It doesn't come anywhere from outside.

After anger, fear is the most common negative emotion felt by mankind. It doesn't allow you to relish and enjoy your life smoothly even when you have everything under your possession to enjoy life.

This enemy can't be overcome just by preaching certain sermons from some holy books. We will have to go to its root causes and attack it from various possible angles to eliminate it. To do so we need to understand both the physiology and psychology associated with it.

The present book is an attempt to understand scientifically the various facets of fear and eradicate this ferocious enemy once for ever.

I wish the readers all the best in their endeavour to overcome this deadly enemy.

**M.K. Gupta**
I.U.A.C. (Formerly Nuclear Science Centre)
J.N.U. Campus, New Delhi-110067
Tel: 26892603, 26892601
*E-mail: mkg@iuac.ernet.in*

# Contents

# Fear: Quotes from Great People

Fearlessness is possessed more often by the so called bodily weak, the poor, the not so healthy and the not so learned. It is a spiritual force. It is a characteristic of the soul and not of the body.

***—M.K. Gandhi***

The greatest fear to a man in this world comes from himself and not from any outside source.

***—Swet Marden***

Fear can exist only in the absence of God. It has no business when you are in the midst of God.

***—The Mother***

The only place where fear can exist is in your mind. It has no other residence.

***—Swami Sivananda***

Fearlessness is essential for the acquisition of all other noble qualities. Truth, love and *ahimsa* will be absent without fearlessness.

***—M.K. Gandhi***

First of all let me assert my firm belief that the only thing we have to fear is fear itself—nameless, unreasoning, unjustified terror which paralyses all our efforts to convert retreat into advance.

***—Franklin D. Roosevelt***

He who strikes terror into others is himself in continual fear.

***—Claudian***

To conquer fear is the beginning of wisdom.

***—Bertrand Russell***

The easiest thing in the world—worry and fear and the most futile.

***—Robert Power***

The only fear permissible is the fear of God and fear of doing evil and that is really fearlessness.

***—M.K. Gandhi***

It is not the work that kills men, it is worry and fears. Work is healthy; you can hardly put more upon a person than he can bear. Worry and fear are like rust on a machinery. It is not the revolution that destroys the machinery, but the friction due to rust.

***—Beryl Pfizer***

We invite what we fear because fear is an acknowledgment of weakness and unprotection that offers easy invitation for invasion by the things we fear.

***—Bacon***

Fear after hate is the most destructive emotion. It breaks down the nervous system and undermines the health. It also renders happiness and peace of mind impossible. Fear gives rise to worry and those who worry are living in hell.

***—Austen Riggs***

One who seeks the transformation and is entering the path of *Yoga,* must become through and through fearless, not to be touched or shaken by anything whatever. One of the uses of the blows and knocks you receive on the path of *Yoga* is to rid you of all fear.

***—The Mother***

When one is free from attachment to wealth, reputation, family, body and surrenders himself to God, fearlessness will come of its own accord.

***—M.K. Gandhi***

Fear has no existence of its own. It is only a creation of your wild and uncontrolled imagination.

***—Swet Marden***

Nothing in life is to be feared. It is only to be understood.

***—Marie Curie***

Fearlessness should mean complete absence of all the fears—fear of death, fear of physical assault, fear of hunger, fear of insult, fear of public criticism, fear of ghosts, fear of someone's anger etc. Freedom from these and all other fears is fearlessness.

***—M.K. Gandhi***

❑❑❑

1

# Fear: Your Uninvited Guest

There is a fellow who lives with you day and night. He sleeps with you, he wakes up with you. He goes to office with you. He eats with you. He travels with you. Possibly he is sitting with you even now as you read this book. Look around and see if he is there. In the evening when you lose yourself in some beautiful park or in a swimming pool for a while, you temporarily forget this fellow. But all of a sudden when you look around, you again find this fellow at your side.

Can you name this fellow which is your constant companion all day long? It is none other than **'FEAR'**. You have given him so much power that he has now become your master and enjoys full authority over you. You, like a puppet, move

*Fear is one of the deadliest enemies of mankind*

around him as a subordinate moves around his Boss, inspite of the fact that you hate him and want to get rid of him.

Fear is one of the greatest enemies which robs us of all our joy, contentment and peace. Fear gradually eats us and practically converts us into a slave. **Our worries and fears about the future prevent us from experiencing the joy and happiness which exist here right now.** We must conquer our fears if we are to enjoy our life to the fullest. Our search for fulfillment in our life can be successful only to the extent that we understand and overcome our fears.

*Fear swallows us and finally destroys us like a dragon*

What is this dragon called fear? Fear is really the anticipation of loss or harm to one's sense of 'I-ness' or ego. **This loss or harm may be physical but more often it is psychological.** It may involve the person himself or the other persons or objects to whom he is emotionally attached and identified such as his family, friends, house, car, job, status, name, fame etc. So fears are tied with perceived uncertainties associated with loss, agony or pain.

❑❑❑

2

# Brothers and Sisters of Fear

There are many other emotions which can't be exactly called 'fears' but they are similar to fear in nature. They can also be called disguised forms of fears. Freedom from fear presupposes freedom from these emotions also. Let us briefly understand about these harmful associates of fears.

## Anxiety

It is a kind of apprehension about something you are waiting eagerly and excitedly. For example you may be anxious about your examination result, about your child's admission in a particular school, about the engagement of your colleague's daughter or about the announcement of your promotion.

Sometimes people have 'free floating anxiety' also when there is no identifiable reason for this. This happens in certain types of persons in whom the general level of arousal remains high due to excess of adrenaline hormone in the blood and overactivity of sympathetic nervous system.

## Nervousness

It is generated out of the feeling of self inadequacy, e.g. whether you will be able to face certain situation; whether you will be able to handle that challenging assignment; whether you will be able to answer all the queries in the meeting etc. etc.

It is different from the fear in the sense that here nobody is threatening your psychological ego or physical survival. **It is generated out of your own feelings of self inadequacy and generally indicates a lack of self confidence in you.** For example you may feel nervous while facing an interview board. You may feel nervous while facing your boss. You may also feel nervous when you are asked to deliver a speech.

## Worry

Like anxiety and nervousness, worry is not the result of facing some specific situation. It is a generalized syndrome which hangs more or less all the time in one's mind. The worrier knows what he is afraid of and what is causing trouble to him but he just can't let the mind rest. The worrier focuses upon the feared object all the time and can't let that fear out of his thoughts. He dwells upon it, thinks about it all the time and finally he himself falls to sickness.

**So while anxiety and nervousness are a short term phenomena generated out of a sudden and specific stimulus appropriate to flare the emotion, worry on the other hand is a long term condition.** Moreover the degree of arousal of

the body and mind during emotions of anxiety and nervousness is quite high (although for a short duration) while the degree of arousal of the body and mind in case of worry is moderate although extending for a longer time.

## Phobia

Phobias are exaggerated and unreasonable fears which a normal person (without phobias) will not fear but a phobic person would do. We will discuss about this condition in de tail in a separate chapter.

❑❑❑

3

# Types of Fears

The list of fears is endless. There may be as many fears in the world as the number of stars in the universe. You can go even to the extent of fearing yourself. However, it will be appropriate to list out some common fears which all of us come across sometime or the other in our life's journey.

- Fear of failure in an examination or in a project or in a game
- Fear of rejection and disapproval by others
- Fear of accident
- Fear of death
- Fear of being shot or murdered by a terrorist or enemy
- Fear of being robbed
- Fear of losing the job
- Fear of being killed in a bomb blast
- Fear of attack by animals
- Fear of insult & misbehaviour by others
- Fear of criticism/comments in your work by others
- Fear of public speaking
- Fear of getting dreadful diseases like cancer, heart attack, paralysis, brain haemorrhage, T.B. etc.
- Fear of separation from children in old age

- Fear of being left alone in old age after the death of one's life- partner
- Fear of extra marital relation by the partner
- Fear of physical assault by an enemy/opponent or some-one
- Fear of molestation and rape
- Fear of natural calamities e.g. earthquake, flood, cyclone, famine, etc.
- Fear of loss in business
- Fear of lagging behind your competitors or colleagues
- Fear of attack by a neighbouring country
- Fear of theft of your belongings and money
- Fear of sexual inadequacy
- Fear of inadequacy of your children compared to other children
- Fear of not getting right bridegroom for your daughter
- Fear of being bankrupt and insolvent
- Fear of kidnapping of your family and/or yourself
- Fear of raid in your house
- Fear of being screened and caught by tax authorities
- Fear of building collapse
- Fear of being caught and burnt alive in a fire
- Fear of monetary inadequacy at the time of need
- Fear of being ridiculed in a social gathering, party or meeting
- Fear of attending interviews
- Fear about your children in not getting suitable employ-ment
- Fear of nuclear war and mass destruction *(mahapralaya)* in the world

- Fear of a comet striking on the earth
- Fear of self-incompetence compared to others
- Fear of your car breaking down in a forest where no help is available
- Fear of ghosts, black magic, *tantriks*, soul possession
- Fear of food adulteration and poisoning while eating
- Fear of singing and acting on stage
- Fear of incapability in handling an assignment or a project or a challenge
- Fear of leakage of harmful gases, radio activity, radiations from a factory or nuclear installation
- Fear of aircrash
- Fear of darkness
- Fear of train accidents of various nature
- Fear of aeroplane crashing into your roof
- Fear of drowning in water while travelling by ship or boat through the sea or river
- Fear of heights
- Fear of enclosed spaces like lifts in buildings
- Fear of socializing
- Fear of being cheated in sale/purchase transactions
- Fear of biased behaviour of bosses in your evaluation and promotion
- Fear of getting a heart attack while walking or driving a vehicle
- Fear of getting punishment after doing an illegal or immoral act.
- Fear of being implicated in a conspiracy

But this long list of fearful situations needn't frighten or despair you. All these fears can be overcome. **Enlightened**

**persons have proved after facing all sorts of situations that existence of fear is in mind only. It has no concrete existence anywhere other than your mind.**

Existence of fear is like a cloud which disappears as soon as the ray of knowledge appears. It is our wrong beliefs and ignorance about the realities of life which give so much power and momentum to these fears. Once the true knowledge dawns and your consciousness awakens from its deep slumber, fears melt away on their own. They (fears) can't stand against an awakened and rational soul.

In fact the following chapters of this book will try to convince you that there is really nothing in the world for which we really need to be fearful. Every experience can be accepted and handled with serenity. There is a cosmic order in the world and nothing has been designed to frighten us. Rather everything has been designed to support our evolution and growth.

**Hence, control of fear is basically control of your mind and imagination and removal of false beliefs anchored in the mind** by knowledge and acceptance of realities of life because, as

*Fear can't dwell in a strong and awakened mind*

mentioned earlier, **fears are nothing but thoughts. So, for removing fears there is no point in fighting with external circumstances and conditions. This fight has to be fought with your own mind only. It is more an internal fight than external.** Fears look for residence in a weak mind only. They can't dare stand against a strong and awakened mind.

❑❑❑

4

# Causes of Fears

On the surface level, several causes of various types of fears can be pointed out but if we go deeply we can convert all these causes into the following root causes:

## Attachment and dependence on external objects

If we are depending on external objects and people for our existence and feeling of self worth, we then experience fear by anticipating the loss of that object. Without a habit of dependency there could be no fear. We would then allow objects and experiences to come and go without trying to cling to them. **But when we feel the intense dependency on something we are inevitably afraid of losing it. Whatever we feel that we must have, is what we fear losing.**

Clinging to the things to which we are attached is like fighting our way upstream, struggling against the basic law of change which pervades our universe. **Rather than squarely facing the fact that everything in life is subject to change, we desperately try to hold on to objects and situations.** With such an attitude, fear is inevitable. But sooner or later we will have to forgo such attitudes which we cling so resolutely. Our new car will eventually rust and break down. Our children will grow and may go out of our home in search of better future and prospects.

To be free from fear we will have to gain freedom from this false clinging. We should realize that we can't depend on the external world for abiding joy and happiness. These things are temporary and won't stay with us for ever. We will achieve freedom from fear when we realize that the source of fulfillment is within us rather than in the external world of objects and events. **When we direct our attention inwards and look there for our joy and satisfaction, we find a sense of fulfillment which always abides within us**.

When we reach this new understanding, we gradually learn to see our external world in a new way. **We can then accept and enjoy what comes our way without clinging to them. Our fears indicate that we are clinging to somebody or something too tightly**. Such a stress can only be relieved by psychologically letting go of our possessive attitude. **When we have learned to let go, we would have found one of the greatest secrets of life for experiencing peace and happiness. Letting go is always accompanied by a feeling of openness and lightness**. We normally fear letting go of our dependency on objects and people, but if we are truly able to do so we will find that what is gained is greater than that which is left behind.

*Just let go of your attachments like a stone falling in a river*

## Feeling of separateness

This is another root cause of our fear—our sense of separateness from each other and from God. We remain unaware of our natural connection with each other and experience ourselves as individual egos separate from each other. **Whatever we see as separate from ourselves, inevitably becomes a source of fear.**

We live in a world of duality which consists of that which is 'me and mine' and that which is not 'mine'. We have created for ourselves a self concept which excludes the rest of the world, an artificial sense of separation. This separation, this duality creates discomfort, disharmony and at times even a feeling of loneliness and isolation.

*Feeling of separateness creates anxiety and discomfort*

The more narrow and more rigidly held is one's concept of identity, the more insecure he will be, feeling small and insignificant in the world, which seems large and threatening. Such a person works primarily to achieve security and his chief concern is self-protection. He looks at himself as an isolated being struggling against the rest of the world. Such a person considers everything which is outside the boundary of his little ego as foreign to him.

## Disbelief in God and cosmic order

This is also one of the major causes of our fear. If we don't believe that there is a ruler of the world who is running the world according to some cosmic order and divine laws, we are bound to be fearful. This is because in such a condition of disbelief in God and a cosmic order, we will tend to think that anything can happen to us at any time in this world without any visible cause or any notice. We will depend upon chance and accident for our survival and safety in this universe. Such an attitude is bound to keep you in a state of constant insecurity and fear. **With disbelief in God, you lose a firm base to hold on in times of crisis and adversities.**

## Feeling of self-inadequacy

Many people think that they can't do what others do. They don't have confidence in their calibre and capability and consider themselves as worthless persons. These people also

*Fear of incapability destroys the fibres of positive thinking*

feel that unless they can do anything perfectly or in a right way, they are no good. They develop an inferiority complex and always remain self-conscious and shaky before others. They always fear rejection and disapproval from others and remain apprehensive of being ridiculed for their incompetence. So they avoid socializing also and suffer the pangs of loneliness. The constant feeling of inadequacy lowers their confidence more and more and thus creates a vicious circle of increasing fear for them. The basic cause for this is lack of trust in themselves which requires to be restored if the fears associated with this factor are to be eliminated.

5

# Removal of Fears

There are several ways to get rid of different fears as mentioned in the following paragraphs. It is desired that we should be sincere and consistent in our approach.

## Know the things you fear

Fear is always of the unknown. When you don't know a thing properly and just imagine about it, your imagination can play havoc. It (imagination) always makes a mountain out of a molehill and presents sometimes such a dreadful picture of the whole thing that you feel terrible. It exaggerates and distorts a danger to you beyond all proportions.

*Our imagination plays havoc with our fears*

Hence the first step and for that matter, a large part of the campaign against one's fears, is to get a complete and thorough knowledge of them—not as they seem to be but as they really are. **The reason that fears are apparently so difficult to defeat is because we allow them to remain vague and shadowy. Like any object in the darkness, they assume dreadful shapes when they are not known properly**. Lay your fears out before you, bring them into light and see them as they really are. They will disappear like mist in front of sun. Fear is like an imaginary ghost which frightens you in the darkness but there is not much to it when you see it in the light.

Most of the things, one fears, never happen and whatever things happen, they also don't amount to anything. It is only our imagination which creates all trouble.

## Do the things you fear

Unless you are willing to take a chance and to expose yourself to the very thing you are most afraid of, you have a very little chance of overcoming your fear. People who have flown in an aircraft a thousand times don't have the same fear as a person who is taking his first flight. Similarly someone who has given many speeches can enjoy what the novice dreads. It doesn't matter what kind of fear it is; whether it is climbing mountains or standing upto your boss; principle is always the same. To overcome the fear **you will have to take the risk which you have been avoiding all through and finally do the very thing you are afraid of.** And you have to continue to do this exercise till such time when the fear totally disappears. The causes of your fear leap on you again and again until you overcome fear. It is a natural law that the more you fear a thing, the more it frightens you. However if you don't fear and stand before it untouched and indifferent, the opposite happens and the fear goes away from you.

Some people hesitate to do a task with active interest simply because of the fear that they won't be able to do it well or

*Face your fears resolutely*

perfectly. They believe that everything they do must be perfect and they will be considered worthless unless they execute the same perfectly all the times. Please note that for anyone, it is virtually impossible to do something perfectly or even upto the mark at the first time's effort. Of the millions of complex tasks of which we are now masters, isn't it true that they were all done badly when we attempted them initially and they were only improved gradually as we continued to do them.

**Practically anything of value requires that one takes a risk of failure or being rejected**. This is the price we all must pay for achieving the greater rewards lying ahead of us. To take risks means you will succeed sometime but never to take a risk means that you will never succeed. Life is filled with innumerable risks and challenges and if you want to get away from all these, you will be left behind in the race of life ending up finally in extreme frustration and depression. A person who can never take a risk can't learn anything. For example if you never take the risk to drive a car, you can never learn driving. If you never take the risk of being rejected, you can never have a friend or partner. Similarly by not taking the risk of attending an interview, you will never get a job.

Hence no matter how badly or insignificantly you do a thing, go on trying the thing you are afraid of. Are you afraid of appearing on stage? Then get on a stage and try your best, no matter how poor it is. Are you afraid of speaking in public? Then don't lose any chance of speaking. First you may try speaking to small groups and later to large gatherings. Get up in public gatherings and ask questions to the speaker. Don't care too much whether or not you are doing well. Do you feel awkward at parties and social gatherings? Then instead of allowing yourself to become an introvert or more afraid, try to go to more parties and attempt light chatter and mingling with the people regardless of how badly or inadequately you socialize. Sooner or later you will get to the point where you will feel more and more comfortable mingling with the people and you may even get to the point where you enjoy it. But you must attend more of them, no matter how badly you are faring currently. To do otherwise is to invite more fear and retreat from the activity.

To conclude, **please remember that avoiding fearsome situations is not the solution to remain free from the tyranny of fears.** This will lead to more discomforts of other kind which will be more unpleasant than facing the original fear. Discomfort connected with overcoming your fear has an ending whereas the discomforts and frustrations that you will have if you don't face your fears can go on until you die.

## Don't identify yourself with the dangers

One of the reasons why fears overwhelm us is that we normally identify ourselves with dangers and become one with them.

You should treat the dangers coming to you as something different from you and not a part of you, having only temporary association with you. **Observe your dangers from a**

**distance like a spectator. See them coming to you and gradually passing away.**

When you can so witness your dangers like a distant observer, dangers become smaller than you and you become bigger than your dangers. Hence although dangers will be there, yet you will remain unaffected because **you have shifted yourself on a plane of awareness from where dangers can be distinctly observed and manipulated.**

## Fear exists in past and future only. It can't exist in the present

As mentioned earlier, fear occurs due to a perceived probability of loss or pain. It is important to see that when this probability becomes a reality, fear gets transformed into depression, or anger or even relief. **Fear only exists within the confines of anticipation, it can't exist within the direct experience of the event itself. It disappears when the actual event that was feared takes place**. The anticipation of harm in experiencing fear is normally based on some past experience; that past memory of pain is recalled and projected into future. However, sometimes emotion of fear arises purely because of the self-preservation instinct of lower mind.

Thus we can see that fear has something to do with the past and future but it doesn't really exist in the present. **This time-dependent aspect of fear provides us the key to the elimination of fear.** Thus if we can control the mind's tendency to anticipate and run towards future and train the mind to

*Learn to bring yourself again and again into the present moment by practice of breath awareness*

always remain centered in present moment, we can control and eliminate fear. Many simple meditative practices, e.g. breath awareness can help us increase our ability to remain in the present moment and reduce our wandering into future or past.

In fact, as your consciousness grows, you will realize that **emotion of fear is quite distinct from object of fear**. It is possible to perceive danger and take self-protective measures without experiencing fear. **Fear is felt either before or after the fearful event has passed but it is never in the present because in the present you are busy confronting the danger and there is no time for thinking or imagination and fear is the product of your thinking or imagination only.**

## Experience your inter-relatedness with others

We are all a part of this overall creation of God. We are not separate from each other and in turn we are connected to God. This realization of this inter-relatedness allows us to remove our false sense of separation which produces a great deal of loneliness, insecurity and fear. Our relaization of interrelatedness with each other creates a feeling of openness and lightness, a sense of fearlessness and ease. As our sense of separation between ourselves and others becomes less and less acute, we begin to work for the common benefit, for 'all of us' rather than for 'me and mine'. There is a new sense of harmony with everyone which was absent when our identity was constricted and narrow. We realize that the isolation which we felt earlier was not real but a misconception and illusion based on our ignorance of our true identity.

With the expanded identity we begin to act from a sense of fullness and inter-relatedness. We now view ourselves as intimately connected with the whole and working for the greater benefit of the whole. We see ourselves as one cell in the large body of humanity. In this state, the idea of working and living for only ourselves seems quite absurd.

## Don't think constantly about the things you fear

**To be upset by a thing, we have to be thinking about it. It is impossible to be fearful about something unless you are thinking about it.** If your thoughts are on something pleasant rather than your fears, you can't be disturbed, no matter what that fear is. Suppose you are thinking about a delicious meal or a football game instead of your court case, you won't feel disturbed because your thoughts are elsewhere. Emotions always require the base of thoughts for their existence. It is the same thing when you turn your eyes from something unpleasant, then you are not able to see it. You can look in only one direction at a time. So is with your thoughts. If you are feeling uncomfortable what you are thinking about, you can focus your thoughts elsewhere.

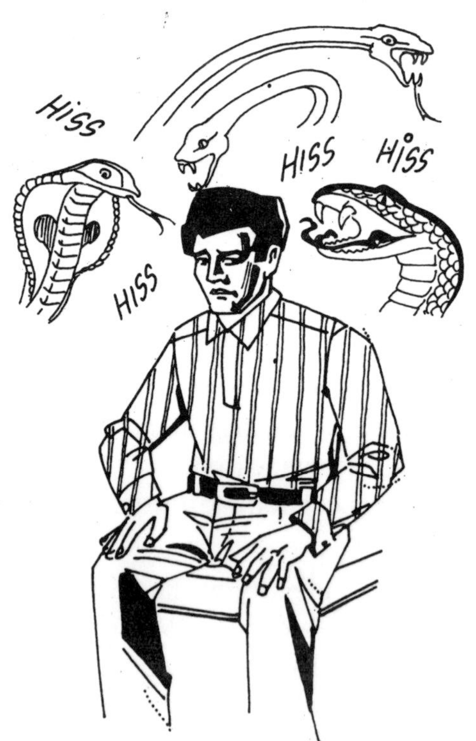


*Don't think constantly about things you fear*

Turning away our thoughts from fears is not the final solution of eliminating fears because it is simply evading the problem but not solving the problem. But often when nothing works, it is a great deal better to distract yourself and get your mind off the situation rather than to dwell upon it all the time.

## There are many more dangers in life than the ones you are fearing, so be rational about your fears

Although you may have picked up a few dangers in life in your imagination and will be constantly fearing their materialization, yet you are ignoring a hundred other dangers around you which are a great deal worse than the ones you are presently focussing upon. If you are to be consistent about your fears, then you should also worry about an aeroplane dropping on your house, a comet striking on earth, an atomic bomb blast by some country, an earthquake, a house collapse, food poisoning in a restaurant, being shot by a terrorist on the street, being robbed in the house by dacoits, an accident by a careless and speeding bus driver, a heart attack while sleeping etc. etc.

In fact the possibility of occurrence of unpleasant things to us exists everyday of our lives. We get up and haven't the foggiest notion of what painful things might happen to us today. I and you can't eliminate all the dangers of life.

**But does this mean that we should focus upon all possible dangers at all times. Don't we have any faith in our ability to survive any crisis. Don't we have any faith in God, ruler of the world**. Once we have done our bit by taking normal desirable precautions about the perceived dangers in our vicinity, we should leave the rest on God.

By constantly dwelling on the dangers of life, you convert them into greater dangers which continuously erode you mentally and physically whether they actually materialize in your life or not. **You should assert that nothing outside of you have the power to upset ycu unless you allow it to do so.**

## Don't make a catastrophe of life's situations

We can't feel fearful about a situation unless we say to ourselves that it is a catastrophe or a life and death situation. If you can persuade yourself that the issue you are dealing with is not really all that serious, then you are bound to calm down. But if you continue to tell yourself that this is the most important thing in life and world will end if this thing happens, then you are bound to remain anxious and disturbed.

Fortunately most of the events in our life are not catastrophic. If we look at our fears carefully and allow sometime to pass by, we will realize that we are not in such a bad shape as we thought initially.

Experience of thousands of enlightened men who themselves faced many storms in life have also proved that there is nothing in this life which can be called terrible or unbearable. Every experience can be accepted and handled with serenity and detachment. It is only when we start taking things unduly serious and giving them more weightage than what they deserve that fears start dominating us.

*For some people facing an interview is a catastrophe*

If you can learn to view things from a distance with a larger perspective maintaining some separation between you and the things, you will find that things are not as terrible as you imagined them from a narrow perspective.

***How to decatastrophize situations:*** If you have the habit of making catastrophe of the various situations and thereby making yourself fearful and upset, then you must learn how to decatastrophize any such situation so as to bring yourself back to a fearless state. To decatastrophize any situation you must ask this question to yourself—**Is this thing so important? What is the worst which can occur if this thing happens?**

For example suppose you are feeling fearful and anxious about an interview you have to appear tomorrow. Just ask yourself what it is that you are feeling so nervous? Is it because you are afraid that you won't be able to reply all the questions? How does it matter if you are not able to reply their (interviewers) questions? At the most you won't be selected. So what? Heavens will not fall. You will not become a beggar on the street. If you are afraid that interviewers will consider you a fool then what will happen even if they think so. There are many fools in the world including greater fools than you. Is it going to make any difference to the world even if you are a fool? Will the world become standstill because of this fact? Then why are you so perturbed?

So this way **by questioning and challenging your fears you can decatastrophize any situation. Nothing is that important.**

## Everything which happens has a reason. Nothing happens by chance or accident

Normally we develop the feelings of fear because we assume that any mishappening or calamity may fall on us any time all of a sudden. But remember **nothing happens by chance or accident in this life. Our life and infact the whole universe**

*The world is governed by a cosmic order*

**is governed by some divine laws. Nobody can overstep these laws.** These laws are operated and implemented by Almighty God personally with hundred percent precision. Hence there is no scope for injustice. **We, due to our ignorance, may apparently feel some calamity as an injustice to us but it is never so.**

So this assurance should eradicate our fear to a considerable extent that whatever will happen to us in life will be according to some law and it will be with the knowledge of God. Nothing will fall on our head just like that. This law justifies various situations in our life on the basis of various cuases which we have created in the past. Every cause leads to an effect and every effect results from a cause.

Hence instead of dreading various sad events which may appear in our life, we should face tham with a welcome attitude and allow their effects to smoothly pass by us. You may learn not to be affected by whatever happens to you and make your mind independent of outside circumstances and conditions. If we oppose adversities and generate irritation and resentment in facing them, *then instead of allowing their effect to dissolve, we generate fresh causes which will create more troubles for us in the future.*

## Don't think about mishappenings and dangers in your life; just face them as they come

By the law of psychic attraction whatever we constantly fear, we actually attract those conditions and circumstances towards us and thus make our prophecy self fulfilling. Hence one shouldn't constantly dwell and focus on the possible future mishappenings. To quote an example, don't think what will happen if I get cancer? 'What will happen if my children leave me alone in old age? What will happen if I lose my job?' and so on. In fact as already explained earlier, most of these things are not likely to happen to you. They are just constructs of your doubtful mind and wild imagination. But by your constant thinking and fears about them, you might attract them towards you and make them happen to you as a reality.

Hence, instead of thinking, just go on facing dangers as and when they come to you. Even if you believe that you will feel pain or suffering at the time of facing the danger, suffer that pain only at the time of the actual incident. Why do you want to suffer that pain now and throughout life in your imagination? A philosopher has very rightly written the following lines for those who were afraid of the pain of death:

> "Even if you believe that death is painful; why do you want to suffer that pain throughout your life? Die only at the time of death. Why do you want to die every moment of life in your imagination?"

## Imagination increases the fear manifold

**In fact, actual mishappenings are never that fearful and painful as our imagination about them.** It is our imagination which exaggerates everything beyond all proportion and prevents us from seeing the reality.

You will yourself realize that at the appropriate moment you are able to face any danger which comes to you and even overcome it as the time passes. It is only your imagination which holds you back from mustering the necessary courage and keeps you dreaming about all negative consequences.

Hence, in your thoughts think only positive and good things happening to you. **Negative things or mishappenings in life should only be faced and not thought.**

In this connection, I would like to pen down the quotes of two great visionaries.

"When you dramatize misery, you make it a hundred times worse. The actual misery will be much less. When you grow spiritually, you don't dramatize a calamity before it happens, you simply face it with a clear, free and energetic mind."

—Swami Jyotirmayananda

"The accident is not as terrible as you feared. The hill is not as steep as you thought before you began climbing.

Hence, adopt a hopeful, confident state of mind. Then the trouble is half overcome before you start."

—Swami Sivananda

## Adversities in life always come along with solutions

This knowledge should also lessen your fear to a considerable extent that whenever difficulties come to us in life, their solutions also come along with. We are never given a burden which we can't bear. If you can look back upon your life, you will surely find that although you were trapped in many problems in your life yet you could always find some solution or the other. It was never that you got stuck to a problem for ever and couldn't go beyond it. So what makes you think that in future it wouldn't be so?

Moreover, as explained earlier, the various difficulties and adversities you undergo in life have a reason and purpose. They come to teach us certain lessons and to strengthen those aspects of our personality where we are lagging. **In the apparently looking cruel and adverse circumstances of life is hidden the infinite mercy of God.** In fact if you ponder over deeply, you will find that **everything which happens to you is for your good only.** Moreover no problem or difficulty is permanent. After serving their necessary purpose, they all will pass away.

Knowing the above truths and benevolence of God in allotting various problems to us, we should set aside our fears once for all. Moreover we should develop the confidence that with the help of our higher mind and Almighty God we can overcome any adverse situation in life no matter how serious it is. You should keep your mind always in a master's position to tackle any situation and treat the situations of life as your servants. **No situation or problem of life can be above you.** It must bow down before a strong and determined mind.

## Overcoming fears of ghosts, black magic, soul possession and other psychical influences

Incidents of ghosts, black magic, soul possession and various other psychical influences disturb only those persons who themselves invite them by constantly dwelling on these matters and making themselves sensitive to them. The more you think and fear these things, the more they are attracted to you. This is the law of psychic attraction. **So if you want to remain immune to such disturbances, first of all don't think constantly about these things and secondly, deny mentally that these things can do any harm to you. The denial is the positive neutralizer of any negative psychic influence coming towards you. What you fear is psychically attracted towards you and what you deny is repelled from you. Such is the law of nature. Denial has a great power of self protection.** For the purpose of comparison you can understand it like this that an ounce of denial overcomes a pound of psychic attack directed towards you. I hope you understand that all the above matters fall in the realm of psychic attack and it is the mentally weak, fearful, sensitive person who becomes an easy target of this attack. These things can't touch the mentally and spiritually strong persons.

## Have unshakeable faith in God

Remember that you may take any outward precautions or steps in removing dangers from your life but still you can't guarantee that you are now hundred percent safe. This world or life has so many uncertainties that no matter whatever you plan for your safety, there is always a misstep. It is not within our power to remove all the dangers from this life. In spite of all our precautions, world can run amok any time. Natural disasters, man made calamities, accidents, divorces, change of bosses, someone changing his mind, stocks going down, all are beyond our control. **Our final security is in God only.**

You are never left alone in any adversity. Omniscient and Omnipotent God is always with you in whatever situation you may be. The whole world may leave you but He won't leave you. In fact you should assert that **with God always with me, I am ready to face any eventuality. Let the worst happen and I can overcome that also with His help.**

So instead of dwelling all the time on possible dangers of life, **we should have an unshakeable faith in the benevolence and justice of God that whatever he ordains for our life is right and good for us. No danger can show its face to you without permission of God. God is above all and under His authority nobody or nothing can cross their designated limits.** No sooner you or anybody crosses his limits, immediately a slap comes from God in some form or the other.

To know this you should remove the fear that anybody or anything can just harm you in this world. **Everything has to pass through God before harming you.** With your firm faith in God you can assure yourself to ride over any storm in life.

## Have trust in yourself

Many people have inferiority complex and constantly fear their rejection and disapproval by others. To remove the fear of rejection and disapproval, it is necessary to have trust in yourself. Feel that you are as good as any other person. You can do everything what others can do.

*Have trust in yourself*

It is not simply a theoretical preaching. It is a spiritual truth that all of us have got the same ultimate potential. There is not even an iota of difference. It is only a question of awakening this potential. If you are feeling self inadequate now, it only means that this potential is still lying dormant in you and you have not yet made efforts to awaken it.

To awaken this dormant potential, first and foremost thing is to believe in it and the second step is to just start doing what you feel you can't do. Haven't you seen many times that although before performing many tasks you were a little apprehensive and nervous as to how you will do it; but when you started doing the same you could do it pretty well. This clearly shows that **you are much better and much more competent than what you think and it is only your negative and self defeating thoughts which are holding you back from giving your best.**

❑❑❑

6

# Overcoming the Greatest Fear: The Fear of Death

*It is not the death which is a problem but it is the fear of death which is creating a real havoc.*

***—Epictetus***

*Observe yourself dying. See death coming to you and going. If you can so observe the death from a distance, you have conquered death. Death is now your slave. Now you will die a conscious death and not the mindless death like an animal.*

***—Acharya Rajneesh***

Although death is the most indisputable fact of life, yet most of the people find this fact very hard to digest. In fact it can be doubted whether any other thing will happen to you or not in this life but there can be no doubt about this fact that you will die one day.

Fear of death is no different than other fears of life. **Actual death is never that painful as your imagination about it**. In some cases when you find a person dying a miserable death, it is due to some other factors and not because of the basic nature of death. Have you not seen those persons dying such a peaceful death. They are talking to you and in the next moment you find them slipping into the lap of death. No pain. No tension. You also might have seen many persons whose face radiates peace and joy after death. It is a sign that they have died peacefully. A person who has lived his life righ-

*Death is not as terrible as it appears*

teously and according to the dictates of God slips into death, when the time becomes ripe, as naturally as a fruit spontaneously falls from a tree after gaining full maturity.

Hence death in its true form is a very natural thing and anything which is natural is neither painful nor to be feared. In the words of a great man **"It is impossible that anything so natural, so necessary and so universal as death should ever have been designed by providence as an evil to mankind".**

**In fact much of the fear of death comes from the fact that man always fears the unknown**. Your imagination always makes a mountain out of a molehill and distorts the reality. Hence to overcome the fear of death it is first of all necessary to know the realities about death. **The more correctly you understand death, the more free you will be from the fear of death**.

Death is the separation of your mind or consciousness or soul from the body. Soul which is the real you and gives you the feeling of I-ness, still exists and very much the same as before your death. It is the body which dies and not the real you. The body is simply your possession just like you possess a car, a house. But you are certainly not the car, not the house. You are different from them. Similarly we dwell in our bodies but we are not the bodies. Creater has put us into this body for the duration of our earthly life.

**So after death we are just the same as before except that you don't have a physical body**. Soul now starts life in a new phase of existence which is non-physical while on earth soul lived a life of physical existence by hiring a body. **This change from physical to non-physical existence is as natural as breathing** and we should be as fearless about it as we are about breathing. There is nothing to fear in death anymore than when we lie down to sleep for the night. Do we fear when we go to sleep at night? Do we fear when our body undergoes change from childhood to youth and from youth to oldage. It all happens so spontaneously and naturally. **Actual passing out from the body is not only painless but often accompanied by a feeling of relief from the heaviness of the body; a natural transition never to be dreaded**.

Painless as we know dying to be, it is nature's own process and is arrived at the exact moment scheduled for us by the Creator in His great plan. When will it be for me? Forget it. It is none of our business.

The new world in which we awaken after death is called the Astral World. We discover that still we are our ownselves. Same thoughts and feelings. We have only shed the body. However, we quickly become conscious of the fact that things other than yourself are slightly but definitely different. There are many spheres in this world known as Astral planes. You will go into that particular sphere which you deserve as per the Creator's plan. Nothing can keep you out of that sphere. We will be normally with people of same tastes and degree of spiritual advancement as ourselves, just as we naturally gravitate to and choose suitable associations on earth. You may meet in the Astral your parents, relatives or friends.

This Astral world is not some place far away from earth. It is right here interpenetrating the same physical world. But since it is at a different vibration so there is no interference between the two worlds. Like the physical world, the Astral world also has its own geography and scenery but you on earth can't see them because it is not in physical dimensions. It is in astral dimension. It can be vividly experienced by the dead living in the astral plane. Similarly the Astral world has its own laws and order. No body can break these laws and order. If somebody does that, he suffers the consequences just like on earth. In the Astral world although you don't have a physical body but you do have another body called Astral Body. It is exact duplicate of the physical body except that it doesn't have solidity and weight. It can also be called shadow body. Since you don't have a physical body in Astral, most of the activities there are mental and thoughts and imagination play a vital role there.

Your Astral stay is basically a transition period between two earth lives, a time for rest and self evaluation. This period is used for pondering over what you have done in the past and what are you supposed to do in future. After remaining in Astral for a fixed period as decided by God, you again take birth into a new body. The place and parents of your next birth are all decided by the Creator depending upon your aspirations and your needs. The period of stay in Astral varies from person to person because every person is different. His requirements and his degree of evolution are different from others.

The description given above is a very short description about life after death. Volumes after volumes have been written to unravel this mystery. But for our present purpose this description is enough and should alleviate any fears in your mind about death. **Death is definitely a major change in your life. But this change is for the better and definitely not horrible**

**and miserable as some people wrongly believe**. We have not touched here about the fate of some low level souls who remain earth bound after death because of their acute emotional disturbances and attachments to the earth. They are not able to go to their respective Astral plane for a long time. These souls themselves remain in miserable states and also try to create troubles for those to whom they are related emotionally or by way of revenge. But these wicked or disturbed souls can't touch spiritually and mentally strong persons. They can disturb only those who are mentally weak and fearful and believe that they can be disturbed by these spirits. By such an attitude they give an open invitation to these entities to disturb them. The very fact that you are reading this book and trying to raise your level proves that you do not fall under these category of souls. So you needn't worry at all on this account.

❑❑❑

7

# Physiological Reactions of Fear

When you are under fear, a lot of internal changes in your body are going on. Intensity of these changes depend upon the intensity of your emotion of fear. **Fear is a condition of stress which activates the stress mechanism of the body. Body senses your fear as some kind of threat** and gears up all body functions so that you can take immediate action for 'fight or flight'. Body can't differentiate whether your fear is due to any real physical threat on your life or it is just an imaginary fear, a product of your doubtful and wavering mind. Physical reactions in both cases are just the same. These physical changes are brought about by one branch of autonomous nervous system known as 'Sympathetic Nervous System' (SNS) which gets aroused in such circumstances. The important changes in the body which occur in such a state of mind are summarised below.

- The heart rate increases
- The breathing speeds up
- The stomach produces too much acid
- The liver releases sugar into the blood stream to provide more energy
- The brain becomes more active and the brain wave frequency increases
- The adrenal glands increase the output of adrenaline hormone

- All the postural muscles tense up. Blood supply to them increases
- Digestion slows down or stops. Muscles in stomach tighten up
- The reproductive system stops working
- Saliva production slows down. Mouth dries up
- The skin sweats and there is a decrease in skin resistance
- The pupils of the eyes dilate

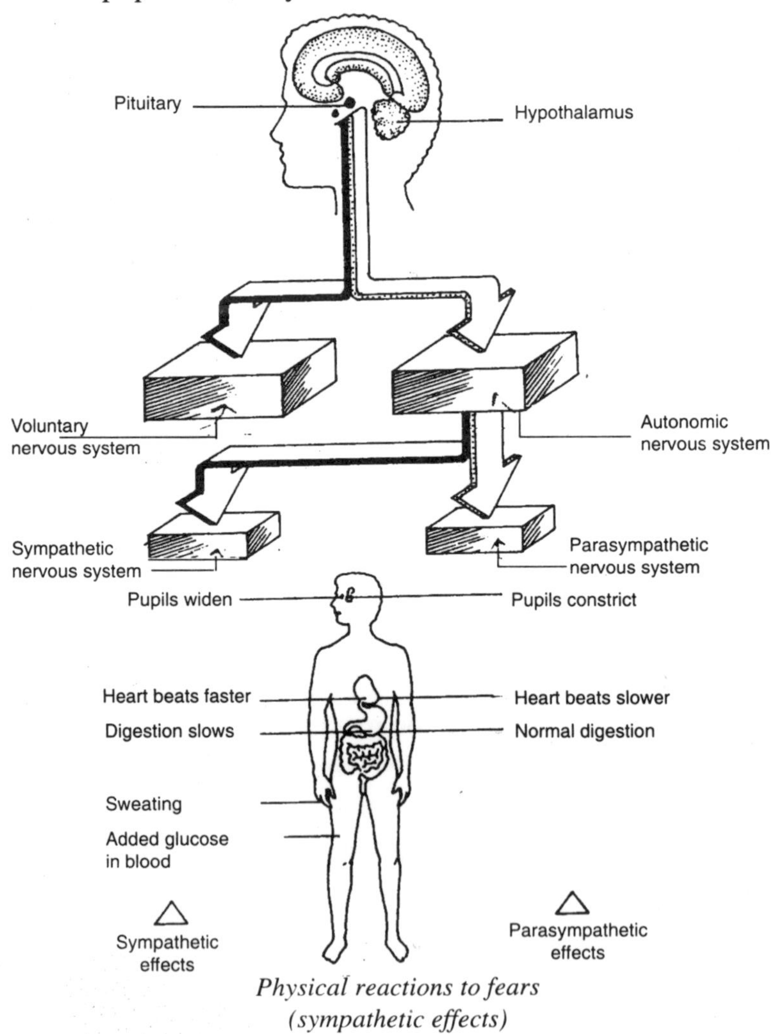


*Physical reactions to fears (sympathetic effects)*

- The hair stands on its end
- Blood pressure increases
- The excretory system closes down
- The immune system stops working
- Tendency of the blood to clot increases
- Stomach upset and diarrhoea may occur
- Decrease in blood flow to the periphery of the body producing effect of cold, clammy hands
- Hand and body tremors
- Blood vessels to the skeleton muscles dilate to allow more blood there
- Bronchial tubes (airways to lungs) dilate to allow more air to lungs
- Red blood cells increase in the blood

Purpose of writing all these physical changes in the body is that you may increase your awareness about them when they are occurring. These symptoms can be easily identified by you than the feelings of anxiety and fear to which you are not even aware of sometimes when they are going on in your mind. Once you notice that these physical symptoms are occurring in you, you can take corrective action to alter these symptoms by various relaxation and other techniques (as described elsewhere in the book). Once the physical symptoms of fear and anxiety are controlled, mental anxiety is also reduced since mind and body are closely interlinked.

Both (mind and body) affect and are affected by each other. They can't function independent of each other.

If the body continues to have these symptoms constantly as happens in free floating anxiety (where the person is in a continuous state of anxiety and overarousal), then the person becomes the victim of a lot of psychosomatic diseases because the body is not able to come to the state of 'Homeostasis' which is very vital if the body is to remain in a balanced and healthy state. Some of the psychosomatic illnesses which can be caused by constantly remaining in stress due to fear are as follows:

***Respiratory disorders:*** (a) Asthma (b) Hay Fever (c) Vasomotor Rhinitis (d) Allergy

***Gastro-intestinal disorders:*** (a) Peptic ulcer (b) Colonic disorders (Diarrhoea, irregular bowel movements)

***Skin disorders:*** (a) Eczema (b) Ringworm (c) Scurvy

***Disorders of muscles and joints:*** (a) Rheumatoid Arthritis (b) Fibrositis

***Endocrine disorders:*** (a) Hyperthyroidism (b) Diabetes mellitus

***Cardiovascular system:*** (a) Essential hypertension (b) Cerebrovascular disease (c) Coronary disease (d) Migraine

***Disorders associated with menstrual and reproductive functions:*** (a) Pre-menstrual tension (b) Menopausal disturbances

Now which disease one will catch depends upon which system is weaker in one's body.

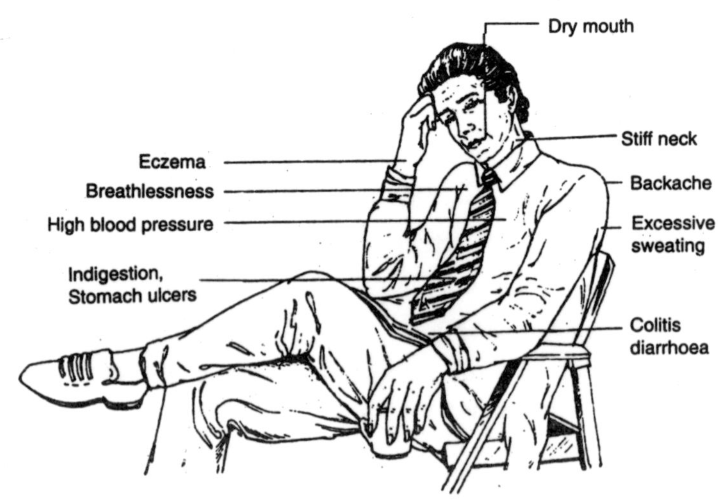


*Disorders due to fear*

Fears and anxieties (and in fact any kind of stress) lower the general resistance of the body making the individual vulnerable to infections as well as other diseases. This comes about because stress interferes with the immune system by reducing the overall number of lymphocytes. Lymphocytes are the cells which attack foreign objects like bacteria, viruses, fungi and tumours as well as tissue grafts and organ transplants. Experiments with artificially frightened animals have also proved the impairment of the immune system and reduced lymphocytes level during fear.

❑❑❑

8

# Behavioural Responses of Fear

Continued and irrational fears affect the general behaviour of the victim significantly. His behaviour no more remains normal and healthy. It becomes a little abnormal. The following tendencies are specifically observed:

## Escape and avoidance

Escape is one of the most basic behavioural responses to fear. The victim normally tries to avoid and remain far from those situations which he fears. For example, a child who antici-

*Some people become escapists as a response to fear*

pates that some aspect of his school will be unpleasant may well try to avoid it by staying at home. Similarly an office going person who has become an escapist by nature may well try to take a lot of holidays and leaves to avoid the threats which he anticipates in his job. But this type of behavioural response only reinforces the fears of the victim more and more instead of helping him to come out of his self made net.

## Consumption disorders

This type of fear related behaviour involves eating, swallowing or otherwise taking things into the body. Smoking, drinking, overeating, undereating and the taking of medicines or other drugs are all behaviour patterns.

*Some people resort to alcoholism to forget their fears and anxieties*

Some people overeat as a response to fear and anxiety and may become overweight or obese. This leads to dissatisfaction with one's appearance and puts a strain on the heart. Conversely fear can also lead to severe loss of appetite and undereating (anorexia). Smoking and drinking are other fear related forms of behaviour. Quantity of smoking and drinking increases considerably in moments of intense anxiety.

## Psychological responses

Under conditions of fears and anxieties our mental alertness and concentration in our day to day work decreases. Our mind keeps on dancing from one thing to another very fast. Our memory weakens. We become confused and fickle minded in taking decisions. Our sense of humour is lost. We also become victims of sleep disorders. We react nervously and irritably, losing control over our reactions. We also become accident prone at home, at work and on the road.

❑❑❑

9

# Phobias

Any amount of knowledge about fear would be incomplete without understanding phobias and the nature, causes and treatment of them. Hence a special chapter on this is included in the book.

## What is a phobia

A phobia is an exaggerated and unreasonable fear about something. If someone reacts to something as if it were dangerous, when in reality it is not, we speak of a phobia. In all of the common phobias the degree of fear the individual experiences is quite out of proportion to the actual danger.

**Phobias are different from fears in the severity of reaction.** With phobias the level of emotional disturbance and the level of physical arousal of the body is abnormally high. People with phobias reach a state of panic whereas those with simple fears rarely do. It is to be noted that things which are really associated with real dangers in life such as driving a car on road, almost never become the focus of phobias. Others such as a spider or a lizard which are generally harmless, frequently become the subject of phobias.

The most important ingredient of phobia is avoidance. A phobic individual is acutely conscious of the possibility of coming into contact with the thing for which he has phobia. For example a person with a spider phobia may avoid going into the bathroom in case there is a spider in the bath.

**Types of phobias:**

There are three main groups of phobias

(a) Specific phobias

(b) Social phobias

(c) Agoraphobia

**Specific phobias** involve distinct objects, animals or defined situations. Some of the commonest specific phobias are of spiders, snakes, insects, birds, dentists, injections, flying, thunderstorms, heights and enclosed spaces.

**Social phobias** include phobias of parties, public speaking, eating in public places and interaction with opposite sex.

**Agoraphobia** is really a set of problems centering around a fear of being away from home by oneself. This fear is often associated with a fear of enclosed places (claustrophobia) and a fear of travelling by public transport. Agoraphobhics become highly panicky if they are unable to get back to home due to any problem. Agoraphobics will often have other phobias

*A harmless insect may become the focus of a phobia for some persons*

*In an extreme case a person may be phobic of his own shadow*

particularly social phobias. The social isolation that agoraphobia leads to, can finally result in loneliness and depression.

## Causes of phobias

There can be many causes which can lead to the development of different phobias:

- If a person, specially in his childhood has undergone any extremely frightening traumatic experience he is likely to develop a phobia against that particular situation or against that type of person or whatever it is.
- If we are told repeatedly by reliable individuals that something is dangerous we may develop a phobia against it.

There is a tendency among children to develop phobias for those things for which their parents (either mother or father) are phobic and repeatedly show their fearfulness for those things. Psychologists have proved that we get many of our emotional responses through observing others.

## Treatment of phobias

Obviously the treatment of phobias will vary depending upon the nature of the phobia. One would not treat the phobia of snakes in the same way as the fear of public speaking. Nevertheless, there are various techniques which can be used either singly or in combination to treat various types of phobias.

***Systematic desensitization*:** This technique involves teaching the phobic person how to relax (see chapter 10) and then exposing him/her to a graded series of feared scenes or objects, starting with the simple scenes. In the case of a spider phobia, the series might start with pictures of spiders, progressing through small dead spiders and ending up with larger

*Treatment of a phobia by systematic desensitization*

live ones. The powerful effect of relaxation will act to neutralize the fear associated with each item in the series. This has proved to be a highly successful method for treating a wide variety of specific phobias.

***Flooding*:** In contrast to the gradual approach of systematic desensitization, flooding involves prolonged exposure to the feared object. This can be done either with real life situations or with imagined ones, in which case the technique is known as **implosion**. These methods work because experience has shown that even very intense fears naturally subside after prolonged exposure of several hours duration.

***Modelling*:** This involves observing non-fearful persons in contact with the feared object, and then imitating the person by the fearful person. This is the process by which most children lose their childhood fears. The fearful person has the opportunity to learn more appropriate ways of behaving toward and dealing with the feared object by observing the other persons behaving in the same situation.

## Self-Help for fighting phobias

Common element in all forms of self help is exposure to or confrontation with whatever it is that you are phobic to. It is important to do it gradually, because sudden and full fledged confrontation might lead to shock and further increase in the phobia also.

In the case of specific phobias such as fear of certain animals, gradual confrontation may be achieved using pictures before moving on to the real thing. The gradual approach may also be used to combat social phobias by first practicing on sympathetic friends and then gradually extending to any social situations.

If you are agoraphobic, try longer and longer trips from home or journeys on public transport, first accompanied by some one and later alone.

Another important tool in fighting with your phobia is that be aware of the physical and behavioural symptoms you develop everytime during a phobic reaction. **This awareness will enable you to apply necessary controls whenever such situation arises again. This is a basic law that once you become aware of what is happening, then that situation loses it power on you and you can regulate the situation like a master instead of being helplessly driven by the situation like a slave**.

In addition to practising all the above mentioned techniques, a phobic person must practice daily conscious relaxation as described in chapter 10.

## Technical names for certain Phobias

1. ***Hydrophobia:*** Fear of water
2. ***Acrophobia:*** Fear of height
3. ***Thanatophobia:*** Fear of death
4. ***Agoraphobia:*** Fear of being in crowded, public spaces (like markets)
5. ***Claustrophobia:*** Fear of enclosed spaces (e.g., being in elevator)
6. ***Acarophobia:*** Fear of small insects
7. ***Achluophobia:*** Fear of the dark

❑❑❑

10

# Medical Approach

When your fears and anxieties have reached to such a stage that you remain intensely fearful and anxious all the time even without any apparent cause then it is not a bad idea to resort to some medical help. This state of the patient in technical parlance is termed as 'Free floating anxiety' and in this state any amount of psychotherapy or preachings won't work at the first instance. For acceptance of knowledge and suggestion, one has to calm down at least to a certain limit. This is where medical science comes to our rescue. But this is to be kept in mind that medical therapy is not to be relied upon

*Some persons have free floating anxiety*

for a long term treatment of the problem because it provides only symptomatic relief and doesn't attack the root causes. **It should be resorted to only as a short term treatment till such time when the patient starts responding to your life changing suggestions and other nature cure methods for relaxation.**

Medical treatment has many side effects also hence it should be used in a restricted manner only when no other thing works to calm down the patient.

## Tranquillizers

The first group of drugs that are used to calm down an anxious mind is known in common parlance as 'tranquillizers'. They act as cerebral depressant. The most common of the modern tranquillizing drugs is the group of chemicals known as 'benzodiazepines'. This includes the well known 'Diazepam' and 'Nitrazepam', better known to many people under their original trade names of 'Valium' and 'Mogadon'. 'Temazepam' is another widely used member of this group, often prescribed as a sleeping tablet because of its shorter action. These drugs have largely replaced the older drugs, of which the most important were the 'barbiturates', because of their greater safety, especially in overdose.

In cases of serious and continued anxiety in response to a serious stress, a short course of a long acting tranquillizer such as 'Diazepam' for a week or two will lower the background level of anxiety sufficiently to be able to cope and deal with stress. Similarly if the anxiety is so severe as to disrupt sleep, which in turn makes your working on the next day still difficult, then a short acting sedative such as 'temazepam' can be useful for a few days.

The long term use of these drugs creates addiction. It can also produce a continuous state of mental slowing and even evidence of brain damage. Particularly in the elderly, the drowsiness and unsteadiness which they cause can result in falls and mental confusion. **Hence the administration of these drugs should be under close medical supervision.**

Another point is when the user tries to cut down these drugs, he or she experiences withdrawal symptoms because of which he or she continues to take them. The only way out of this vicious circle seems to be slow, gradual withdrawal over a long period under close medical supervision. Attempts to cut down too rapidly or 'just take one when I really need them' can do more harm than good.

## Beta blockers

There is another group of drugs which can also reduce the anxiety by affecting the nervous system in another way. These are known as 'Beta Blockers'. Beta-blockers decrease the activity of the sympathetic nervous system. **As already described this part of the nervous system outside the brain is responsible for many of the physical symptoms of anxiety.** Blocking its activity with these drugs stops the rapid pulse and all other symptoms which are related to anxiety which ultimately results in reduction of mental anxiety.

Unlike the other drugs discussed earlier, these are not addictive and they don't act on the brain but on the autonomic nervous system outside the brain.

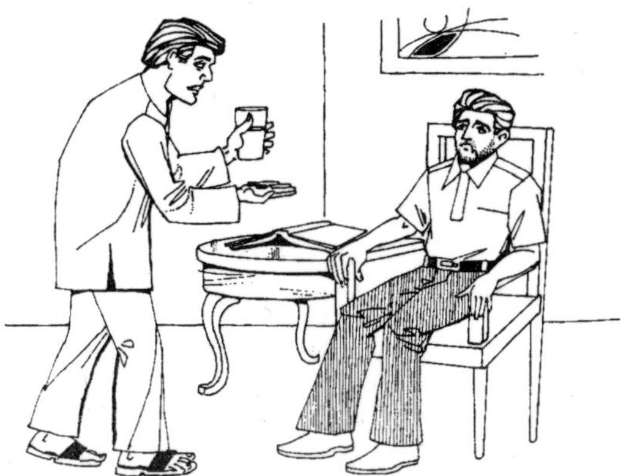

*Medicine can be used only as a short term treatment of fear and anxiety*

❑❑❑

11

# Relaxation Therapy

When a person remains generally fearful and anxious without any clear identifiable cause, it is due to his high general level of arousal. It is related to the type of personality he has.

In such cases it is also advisable for the person to carry out some relaxation exercises to calm him down and to reduce the general level of arousal which always underlies the anxiety. It will be in addition to the constant endeavour of changing one's mental attitudes based on the matter given in earlier chapters.

In relaxation techniques, the aim is to decrease the overactivity of the sympathetic nervous system which underlies your anxiety. Once the physical factors associated with anxiety are brought under control by suitable relaxation techniques, it is difficult to be mentally anxious. There is such a close interconnection between the body and mind.

There are normally three approaches available for relaxation and calming down

(i) Muscular Relaxation

(ii) Breathing

(iii) Meditation

## Muscular relaxation

Almost always when someone is fearful or anxious, his muscle tension is increased. This muscle tension makes you

*Stretching exercises*

further prone to anxiety. By making yourself muscularly relaxed, you can reduce your anxiety level. Muscular tension is best removed by Hatha Yoga stretching exercises. By fully contracting and stretching a muscle to its limit, it comes to a relaxed and balanced state in its resting position. Some of the stretching exercises to loosen your muscles are shown above.

You can remove the tension of your muscles by Aerobic exercises also because the energy bound in the form of tightness of muscles is released and consumed in exercising. Massage is another way to relax tight muscles.

Sitting meditative postures are also very good for calming down your anxiety and nervousness.

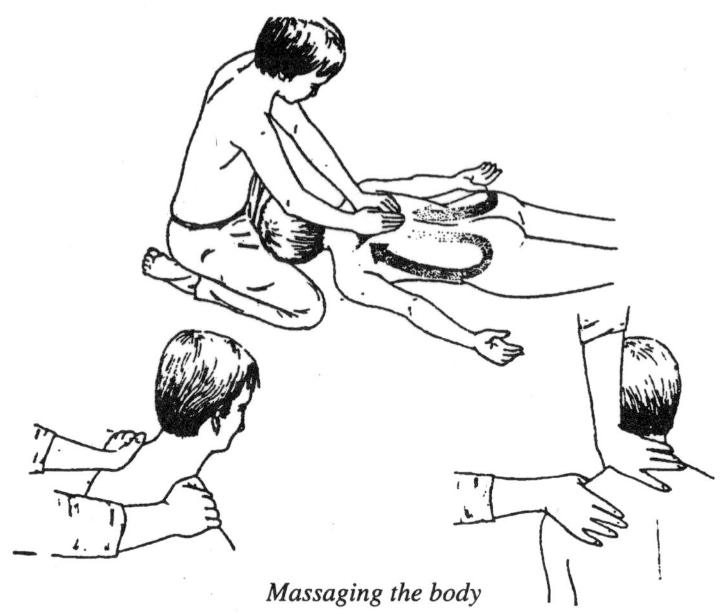

*Massaging the body*

You should sit in any one of them convenient to you for as long as you can sit, making sure that your trunk, neck, and head remain in a straight line so that spine remains in the correct alignment. In yogic parlance these postures help to take 'prana' upwards towards the head which helps in the calming of mind. You can practise *padmasana* or *siddhasana* or *swastikasana* or *vajrasana* or *sukhasana.*

*Vajrasana* *Sukhasana*

There is a very good yogasana called *Shashankasana* which very effectively calms an anxious and fearful mind. It is described below.

Sit in the position of *vajrasana*; inhale and then while exhaling stretch your hands ahead, and bend your body forward from the buttocks. Put your head on the floor. Buttocks shouldn't be raised above the heels while bending. Breathe normally and rest in this pose for as long as you wish. Those persons who are fat, and can't bend easily and touch their head on the floor, they may spread their knees apart while bending.

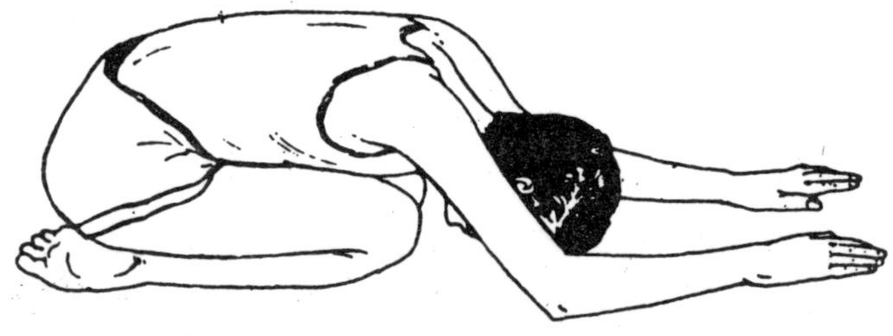

*Shashankasana*

## Breathing

Breathing plays a very key role in relaxing the body and mind. When you are tense and anxious your breathing is shallow, rapid, jerky and irregular. This type of breathing is only limited to your middle and upper chest with no movement of the diaphragm. The relationship is reverse too, i.e. anybody who is habituated to upper chest breathing will tend to remain in a state of anxiety and stress.

When your mind is relaxed, your breathing is slow, deep, even and rhythmic. This type of breathing involves full movement of diaphragm and the breath goes right upto your lower lungs. This is also called abdominal or diaphragmatic breathing.

So whenever you feel anxious and fearful, you can immediately counter this state by starting slow, even and diaphragmatic breathing. To ensure that your breathing is diaphragmatic, just put your hands on your abdomen. With every inhalation abdomen should go up and with every exhalation it should go down. Keep the process easy and effortless. So by learning to control your breathing you can control your anxiety at will.

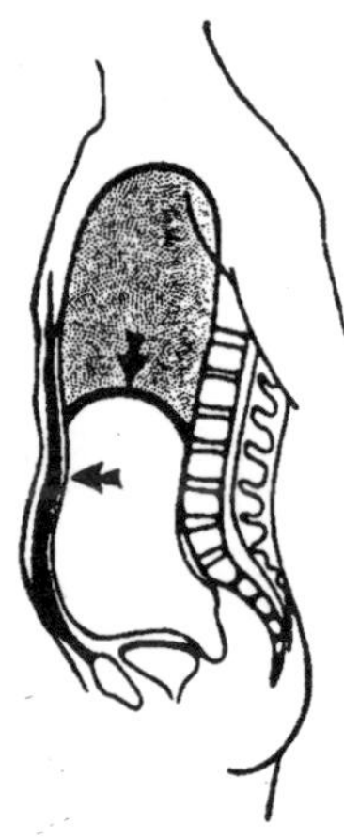

*During inhalation the diaphragm contracts downwards and the abdomen expands*

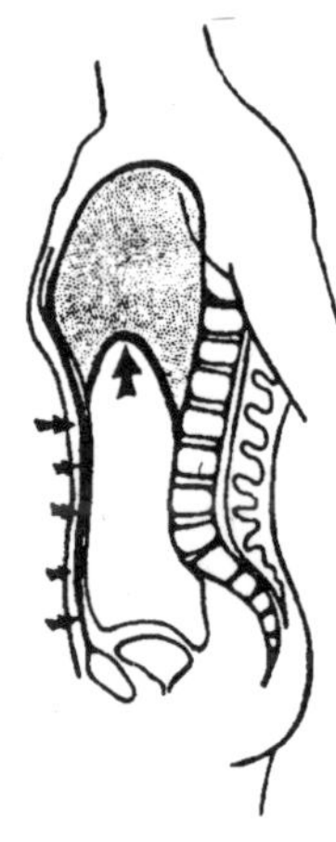

*When the diaphragm relaxes during exhalation the abdomen contracts*

*Nadi Shodhan Pranayama* is also said to be very effective for reducing anxiety and bring balance to your nervous system. This *pranayama* is very helpful in balancing both components of your autonomous nervous system, namely, the sympathetic and para-sympathetic nervous system, and thereby stabilize your mind.

Holding your right nostril, shut with the edge of your right thumb, inhale to a count of eight through the left nostril. Then close your left nostril also with the index finger, and hold your breath for a further count of eight. Release your thumb from the right nostril and exhale to a count of sixteen, keeping your index finger on the left nostril. Then begin inhaling again through the right nostril, reversing the sequence. This is one round. Do more rounds as per your capacity. Retention counts can be gradually increased but the ratio of inhalation and exhalation time should be maintained as 1:2. To keep your exhalation extended as required, you may have to adjust your inhalation, and retention time.

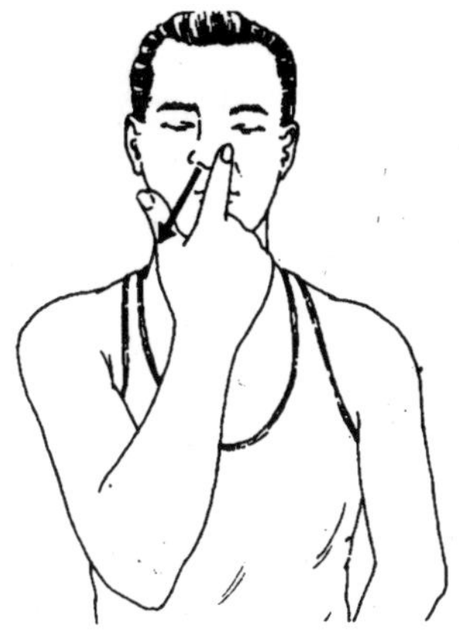

*Nadi shodhan pranayama*

## Meditation

Relaxation by meditation involves the use of mind itself to achieve relaxation. In this method mind is made calm and still by focussing it on some neutral thing. This focus can be a visual object, a sound or a *mantra* being repeated mentally. The beginners usually find it convenient to focus their mind on their breath noticing how abdomen swells during the inhalation and how it falls during exhalation. This breath awareness is good enough for most of the people to achieve sufficient relaxation. Bringing your mind to the perception of a single stimulus immediately puts a break to the inner chatter going in your mind and thousands of thoughts moving across your mind immediately come to a standstill. This is because while you are perceiving, you can't think. Perception and thinking can't be carried

*Meditation*

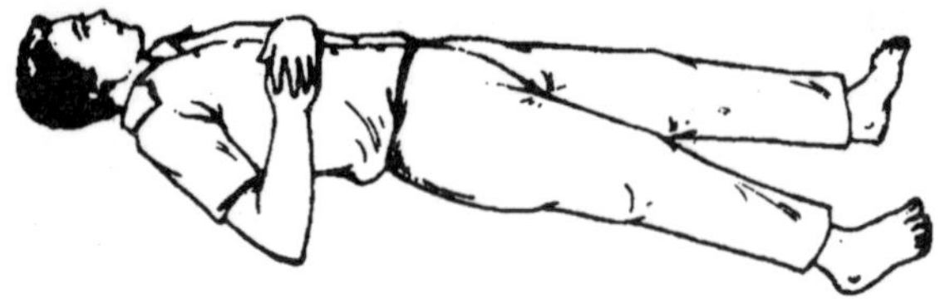

*Breath awareness while lying*

out simultaneously. But while doing this sort of mental relaxation, the body should be completely comfortable, clothes should be loose, posture should be straight and balanced. If there is some discomfort in the body while sitting, it will not allow your mind to focus and calm down. You can also do this type of relaxation while lying in the bed before going to sleep to induce an easy sleep particularly when you feel that you are not able to sleep because of some anxiety.

In addition many other miscellaneous approaches for relaxation and calming down can also be used. For example cold water acts as a great relaxant for an anxious and aroused person. It immediately soothes the frayed and tense nerves.

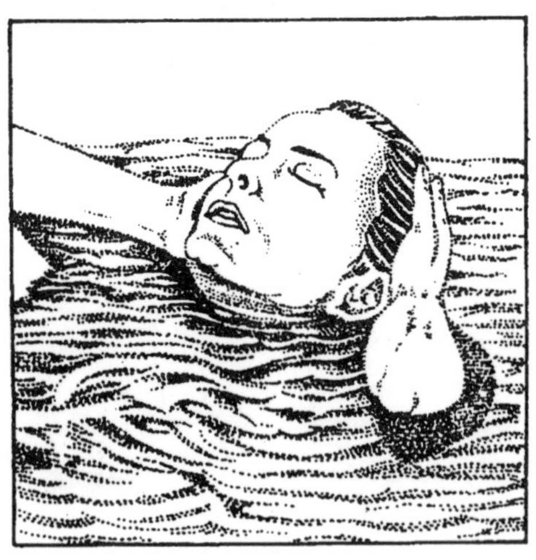

*Relaxing effect of water*

As you gradually calm down by these relaxation techniques, you feel at ease even in the midst of fearful circumstances and you know that your fear will not grow into something that will overwhelm you. When you know you are capable of taking care of your fear, it is already reduced to the minimum, becoming softer and not so unpleasant. You now have the opportunity to go deeper to the source of fear and let it go.

# 12

# Mind Elevating Thoughts

Below are some thoughts which will elevate your mind about the philosophy of life. If you contemplate upon them you will understand the truths of life more closely and your consciousness will expand. Expansion of consciousness spontaneously leads to elimination of fears as a natural process.

1. If your desires are endless, your fears and anxieties will be so too.
2. Our fear of disasters that may never happen robs us off the courage to meet even the common challenges of life.
3. Truth fears no trial.
4. An aimless life is always a miserable life. Every one of you should have an aim. On the quality of your aim will depend the quality of your life.
5. What lies beyond us and what lies before us are tiny matters when compared to what lies within us.
6. Whatever you can do with the association of God, you won't be able to do alone.
7. Time can't be stored like any other commodity. Time not utilized is wasted for ever.
8. You don't know what you can do unless you try.
9. If you want to be big, don't ignore small things.

10. Human affairs would be far happier if the power in men to be silent were the same as that to speak.
11. Desires multiply faster than we can satisfy them.
12. Science divorced from spirituality can lead to catastrophe.
13. Source and solution of all our problems lie within us. Chaos observed outside is the projection of our internal chaos and conflict.
14. The meek man resists none and thereby conquers all.
15. The final say in every matter is of God. The freedom given to you is only in the performing of actions and not in the results.
16. Peace is only found in freedom. It can never be found in slavery or bondage.
17. The way to change the world is not to work upon the world but to start working and introducing changes in yourself.
18. Nothing is that important in the external world. You should be able to forget and cast aside anything at a moment's notice.
19. Man has been given the power to cross over all the tides and storms of life. He only needs to realize this power.
20. A God surrendered person can't remain without God even for a moment. The moment God is away from him, he simply drops dead.
21. No situation in life is permanent. Scenes change fast in the journey of life.
22. If you have failed this time in a work, next time it will be that much easier for you to succeed.
23. Source of all our negative emotions lie inside us. External situations only act as a trigger.

24. Beginning of all big things is small.

25. An enlightened person is a self governed person. He doesn't require any outside rules and laws to control him.

26. Share all your problems, thoughts and feelings with God. With His help you can solve.

27. Every problem and difficulty are temporary. It has to recede or subside after its *karmic* time is over but during that time you have to firmly stand against the problem instead of running away or resenting the problem.

28. Forgiveness is not giving in but letting go of your grudges against someone and becoming free. The other person may not deserve forgiveness but you deserve to be free.

29. One can't reach heaven unless one dies himself. You can't ask somebody to die and show you the heaven.

30. By getting angry, you are indirectly giving the other person the power to disturb you. This switching on and off mechanism of your mood should be in your hand and not in other's hand. How can others disturb you without your permission?

31. Pleasure doesn't remain pleasure if it continues for a long time.

32. Happiness means feeling at ease and at peace with yourself and enjoy whatever comes to you during the journey of life.

33. Nature is God's gift to us. Let us preserve it instead of polluting.

34. The secret of success is not to do what you like but to like what you do.

35. The material world or *Maya* has power to affect you only to the extent you allow it to affect you. If you treat the world as your servant, it can't disturb you.

36. O worldly man! You are fighting for few thousand rupees here & there. Once you conquer your mind, the whole universe will be yours.

37. Science & technology may greatly reduce physical distances and yet the mental & emotional distance between two brothers, between husband and wife may increase. Science may provide us with quick means of communication and yet we may not be in communication with even our ownself.

38. If you can make God your associate in each activity you do, all your actions will become spiritual and pure.

39. An inner illumination that doesn't change the outer life is not an illumination but a mockery of it.

40. Yoga has to enter in each phase of your life rather than restricting itself in morning or evening hours. All life down to the smallest detail has to be divinized.

41. A *bhakta* wears the coating of God around him and **therefore sees everything in terms of God, just like by wearing coloured glasses you see everything in terms of that colour. After wearing the protective coating of God around you, everything will come to you through God. It will touch God first before touching you thus making you completely safe.**

42. When the forces of dynamic will and positive mental imagery coincide, you generate tremendous power, culminating in peak performance.

43. Obstacles in the pathway of the weak become stepping stones on the pathway of the strong.

44. Mind is the most powerful thing in the world. One who has controlled his mind can control anything in the world.

45. The type of environment and circumstances around us only reveal the kind of images and thoughts that we are harbouring in our mind.

46. If you are not big enough to accept criticism, you are too small to be praised.
47. Spirituality means living in constant awareness of God and working in the world from this awareness with total detachment towards worldly things and incidents, except using them as your servant.
48. The degree of your connection with God determines the degree to which he is with you. If you are 10% with Him. He is 10% with you. If you are 50% with Him, He will be 50% with you. If you have fully surrendered to Him, He will be fully with you in all your thoughts feelings and works.
49. The purpose of all *karmas* should be to grow and manifest the essential divinity in man by working for good of all. Material success or failure and earning money by doing *karma* are the very petty outcomes of *karma* and unimportant for a spiritual 'Sadhak'
50. Development of consciousness doesn't consist in accumulating and adding more & more things but rather giving up, letting go and uncovering yourself more & more till you finally come face to face with your real self.
51. In Yoga, it is not important as to what *karmas* you are doing. It is only the attitude with which you do *karma* is important. So it is not the 'what' but 'how' of *karma* which has got meaning in Karma Yoga.
52. Karma Yoga is the art of doing your *karmas* most skilfully while keeping yourself completely free and unattached to the *karma* or its consequences. You enjoy only in the process of work.
53. If you remain simple, you can become a sample for others.

54. Bliss is never attainable in finite life which is characterized by selfishness. Bliss is always in infinite when your self expands to include the rest of the universe.

55. Our inner or spiritual aspect and outer or material aspect shouldn't be in conflict with each other, if properly understood. They should support and complement each other.

56. When we become simple, the world outside also becomes simple. It is only when we become complex with all sorts of desires, ambitions and competition, then the world becomes complex and difficult to understand.

57. Greatest men of the world were the most simple and relaxed in their approach.

58. Mind is like your spectacles on the eyes. If it is dirty, everything outside will look dirty. If it is clear and pure, everything outside will look clear and pure. So although the external world is same yet it looks differently with the type of minds we have.

59. Top of the ladder is never crowded.

60. There is always a huge gap between what we are and what we can be.

61. Once we yield to one desire, the power of other desires to attack on us increases manifold. It is as if we let loose the string by submitting to one desire.

62. When the mind is turbulent, it is away from its centre of consciousness (real self). When it is calm and quiet, it comes close to its centre or true self and enjoys real bliss and peace.

63. Pleasure never satisfies a person. It only leads to a more desperate search for pleasure. Hence the more one pursues pleasures, the more dissatisfied he becomes.

64. One's desire is a disturbance in the calm lake of mind. Disturbance elicited by a desire can't be quenched either by fulfilling the desire or by repressing it. One finds relief only when one gives up the desire.

65. Everything begins with the mind and ends with the mind only. Hence it is the mind which needs to be insulated and strengthened.

66. If your power to satisfy desires increases in arithmetic progression, the power of desires increases in geometric progression.

67. Once you start changing, you find that the world outside is also changing.

68. Working in the world without a meaning or purpose is like getting lost in a dark forest. We must have a centre or reference from which to work in the world.

69. If you try your best to get a thing and still you don't get it, it simply means that you don't need it.

70. Living in the world with a purpose is different from just being alive.

71. If you can just walk towards God, He will run to you.

72. The final perfection and attainment in Yoga is a consciousness in which it is impossible to do anything without God; if the Divine were only for a second to withdraw from you, you would simply drop dead.

73. Both good and bad, happiness and tragedy in life can be used for the development of our character. Don't resent bad while welcoming good. You can grow against an adverse destiny also.

74. An individual's opinion should have greater weight than the opinion of many, if the opinion is sound.

75. Truth will remain truth even if there is not a single follower of it in the world.

76. Live in the world like a mudfish. The fish lives in the mud but its skin is always bright and shiny unaffected by the mud.

77. When the mind becomes enlightened, it doesn't get contaminated with the dirt of the world. It floats detached on the water of the world.

78. One should feel a yearning for God like the yearning of a man who has lost his job and is wandering from one office to another in search of work.

79. If you want to be mad, be mad for God alone.

80. Wherein lies the strength of a devotee? He is the child of God. His devotional tears are his mightiest weapon.

81. Jnana (knowledge) has entry only upto the drawing room of God, but love can enter his inner apartments.

82. Life can't go on without much forgetting.

83. Life is like a mirror. Smile at it and it is charming; frown at it and it becomes sinister.

84. Love endures only when the lovers love many things together and not merely each other.

85. No one has deceived the whole world nor has the whole world deceived anyone.

86. Never was anything great achieved without danger or risk.

87. Death is an art like everything else. You can know a true yogi by the way he dies.

88. Great things are done when men and mountains meet. This is not done by jostling in the street.

89. Our deeds determine us, as much as we determine them.

90. Begin a good thing not with a programme but with an act.

91. When we have gone beyond our individual ego, death no longer exists. It is our ego which creates terror for death.

92. Wake up before death comes and surprises you, in order to die peacefully.

93. There is always a power beside you which is greater than all the odds which can ever come to you in your life time.
94. Those who are inclined to make compromises on wrong things, can never make a revolution.
95. On the quality of our life, depends the quality of our death.
96. You can't build character and courage by taking away man's initiative and independence.
97. The art of progress is to preserve order amidst change and preserve change amidst order.
98. Nothing is permanent but change. Change is nature's mighty law.
99. In a really just cause, the weak conquer the strong.
100. Until the day of his death, no man can be sure of his courage. Death is the final test.
101. Physical bravery is an animal instinct, moral bravery is a much higher and truer courage.
102. Drown not thyself to save a drowning man.
103. Everything in the world has a beauty of its own but not everyone sees it.
104. No doctor is a good doctor who has never been ill himself.
105. In the ignorant society, blind lead the blind.
106. The test of democracy is the freedom of criticism.
107. Chance happens to all but to turn chance into your favour is the gift of a few.
108. Courage is the mastery of fear and not the absence of fear.
109. Fortune sides with him who dares.
110. A journey of thousand miles begin with a single step. The beginning is the most important part of any work.

❑❑❑